Written by Michael Bond
from ideas by Lesley Young
Illustrated by Ivor Wood

Published in 1978 by
The William Collins+World Publishing Co.
Cleveland and New York

ISBN   0–529–05498–1
Library of Congress Catalog Card Number
78–54612

Printed in Great Britain

Library of Congress Cataloging in Publication
Data
Bond, Michael.
    Fun and Games with Paddington.
    SUMMARY: Paddington the Bear presents
a variety of activities involving Fortune
Telling, Baking, Gardening, Photography,
Games, Crafts and Amusements.
1. Creative Activities and Seat Work
    (1. Amusements)
    I. Wood, Ivor
    II. Title
GV1203.B668   1978   790.19′22   78–54612

FUN AND GAMES WITH
Paddington

Michael Bond

Pictures by Ivor Wood

Collins

32 Windsor Gardens
Lundun.

Dear all.
This is a book for all those who like Kartoons, Marmalade, making things out of skraps, reading foyrtunes in the bottom of tea-cups, and

← I'm afraid I made a bit of a mess there when I tried to read my fortune in the bottom of a cocoa-mug, so there is only reelly room to say I hope you enjoy the fun and games in this book as much as I did when I tested them.

Yores sinseerely
Padingtun

P.S. Mrs Bird says 'Don't forget to cleer up any mess you may make afterwords — otherwyse you won't be very poppular (neither will I!)

Contents

Canada

United States
of America

Britain

Europe

Paddington

Africa

Pacific Ocean

South America

Peru

Atlantic Ocean

Aunt Lucy

8

Arctic Ocean

Russia

India

China

Japan

Indian Ocean

Australia

New Zealand

Paddington's World

9

PADDINGTON IN FOCUS

Paddington was delighted to receive a camera as a special birthday present from the Browns. He was eager to try his paw at photography at once, and take lots of snapshots to stick into his scrapbook to send to his Aunt Lucy in Peru. He soon found, however, that there is more to taking photographs than just aiming the camera and pressing the button. Here are the very first pictures that Paddington took. You can learn from his mistakes, and improve your own photography by studying these pictures.

A lovely picture of Mrs. Bird's feather duster and right foot! This was to have been an action shot of Mrs. Bird spring-cleaning. Unfortunately Paddington was too slow, and Mrs. Bird has almost cleaned her way right out of the picture!

Mr. Brown relaxing in a deckchair with his newspaper. He seems to have huge feet and a tiny head because Paddington held the camera far too close to the ground.

Jonathan has a sunflower growing out of his head! No, he hasn't let Paddington's gardening hints on page 16 go to his head. The sunflower is growing behind him; Paddington should have asked him to move to one side a bit; then we would have seen them both properly.

11

A very nice portrait of Mrs. Brown is ruined because Paddington had the tip of his paw in front of the lens when he pressed the button.

A picture of Mr. Gruber outside his shop. It may look like midnight, but it was actually broad daylight. Paddington forgot to take the protective cover off his camera lens.

A group of Paddington's friends from the Portobello Market. The trouble was, nobody wanted to be left out. To make sure of getting everyone in, Paddington moved much too far back. Now we cannot recognize anyone!

Mr. Curry. No, he wasn't trembling from fear that Paddington might ask him to *pay* for the portrait. Paddington (and the camera) moved as he pressed the button with his paw.

This artistic still-life 'cocoa and buns' was ruined because Paddington didn't hold the camera straight. (Paddington says he was in a hurry to finish the photograph before the cocoa got cold.)

Most cameras today have an automatic timer so that you can take a picture of yourself. You set the camera, and then you have about eight seconds in which to take up your position. Unfortunately, Paddington didn't look through the viewfinder first to make sure all of him would be in the picture.

Don't worry, Judy hasn't got mumps! Her face is distorted because Paddington held the camera much too close to her.

A perfect picture of the Brown family. At least Paddington is a bear who learns from his mistakes!

PADDINGTON'S HOLIDAY

One day Paddington was out shopping when he saw a notice in a shop window.

Paddington liked a bargain, and it sounded like a very good value indeed.

So he decided to investigate the matter straight away.

'A very good choice, sir,' said the assistant. 'I can just picture it all.'

'Close your eyes, and I will tell you about it.'

Paddington was tired after his shopping and he needed no second bidding.

'On the first day,' said the man, 'I see you in Paris, climbing the Eiffel Tower.'

'On the second day—Spain, with a visit to a bullfight.'

'Then Venice, with a romantic trip round the canals on a gondola.'

'Followed by climbing the Matterhorn in Switzerland; ending up on the fifth day . .

. . . skiing in Austria. Only two hundred pounds! How's that for a bargain?'

Paddington rubbed his eyes. 'I'd sooner have one day in Brightsea!' he exclaimed.

'It's a lot cheaper and much, much safer. I shall go with Mr. Gruber.'

'If you close your eyes I'll tell you all about it.'

'I can just picture it all!'

SUNFLOWERS

As you probably know, Paddington was brought up by his Aunt Lucy in Darkest Peru. In some parts of Peru, huge plants sprout up and grow to great heights without any help from anyone. So when Paddington came to live with the Browns at 32 Windsor Gardens, he was very interested to see Mr. Brown's garden. Mr. Brown spent quite a lot of time there at certain times of the year, doing various important-looking things with tools, canes and bits of twine. And yet the plants never grew as tall as the ones in Peru which were left to their own devices. Paddington thought easily the most impressive-looking plants were Mr. Brown's sunflowers. He thought they were very well named as they reminded him of the bright Peruvian sun. Mr. Brown said they were very easy to grow too. If you have a garden, why not try growing some for yourself?

Sunflowers are best planted against a wall or a fence, in a sunny, sheltered place. They are grown from seed. You can buy a packet of seeds at a gardening shop; their proper, Latin name is *Helianthus* but just ask for the giant, old-fashioned kind. Sow the seeds in the spring in groups of three, 40 centimeters (15 inches) apart, where you want the flowers to grow. When the plants appear above the surface, weed out two of every three seedlings, leaving the strongest with plenty of room to grow. In dry weather, remember to water the plants often. A little liquid manure—which can

also be bought at gardening shops—will make them grow extra strong and tall. When the plants have grown up a bit, it is a good idea to tie them to bamboo canes, driven into the soil beside them, for support. In the summer the sunflowers should grow to a height of two meters (7 feet) or more! They don't have any smell to speak of, which Paddington says is just as well as the flowers are far too far up for his nose to reach! Not only are sunflowers amazingly large flowers, they are 'good value' in other ways too. When they are fully grown, you will see that in the center of each flower is a tight cluster of striped seeds. You can use these in several ways:

1. Store them carefully and plant them next spring for more sunflowers. You will have enough to share among your friends.

2. If you have a hamster as a pet, he will love eating the seeds. You can try eating them yourself. Crack the outer casing, and chew the soft 'kernel' inside. It's quite an unusual taste, and although Mrs. Bird says they contain sunflower oil which will make his fur glossy, Paddington doesn't think they'll ever take the place of marmalade sandwiches!

3. Use the seeds to make an 'everlasting sunflower' to hang on a wall to remind you of summer:

You will need:

A large piece of white cardboard: yellow crepe paper; glue; scissors; thick green poster paint; a pair of compasses and a pencil; sunflower seeds.

What to do:

With the compasses, draw a pencil circle for the flower center, as shown. Paint a green stalk down from the center, and add a few leaves. Leave to dry. Cut out 30 tapering petals (about 12 cm, $4\frac{1}{2}$ ins. long) from the crepe paper. Glue the base of 15 of them round the circle.

Leave to dry. Now glue on the other 15, over the joins of the first 15. Leave to dry. Cover the flower center with glue. Immediately press on lots of sunflower seeds. Gently shake off any loose ones.

You can buy a small plain calendar at a stationery store very cheaply. If you attach this to the bottom of the cardboard with two small strips of ribbon, and add a ribbon loop at the top, you have a lovely sunny Christmas present.

18

AKounts.
Outing to Brightsea with MR GRUBER
Buns
Postcard to Ant Lucy
Emerjency marmalade
dekchare
chokolate Sunday
prezents

This is a page of Paddington's 'Akounts', which he usually keeps safely in the secret compartment of his suitcase. As you can see, it shows his expenses during a day's outing to Brightsea with his friend Mr. Gruber. The outing turned out to be rather expensive, and Paddington was left with very little bun money for the rest of the week. He told Mr. Gruber this over their usual snack of cocoa and buns a few days later. Mr. Gruber was very sympathetic. In fact, he showed Paddington two ways in which he could have saved some of his

Gruber showed him how he could have made presents from something he could get for nothing at Brightsea—pebbles.

Mr. Gruber had a box of pebbles at the back of his shop, which he brought out.
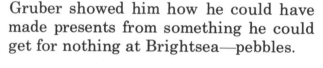
You will need:
thick, bright poster paints; a brush; clear varnish; and plenty of newspapers to spread around to catch any drips.

bun money for other things—like more chocolate sundaes!

A very expensive item on Paddington's list was presents, as he had brought back something for all the Browns. Mr.

The trick is to find pebbles with bumps, which look as if they could be something else. 'I'll show you what I mean,' said Mr. Gruber.

He produced a squat rectangular pebble with a ridge along the top. Paddington watched with interest as he painted four black window frames and a green door on the front, and bright red tiles on top. Then he painted **32** on the front door, and added a small green shrub beside it. He left the background unpainted for a 'stone' effect.

Paddington saw that the pebble had turned into a model of 32 Windsor Gardens, where he lived.

'It's important to leave it until it's dry. Then clean your brush and paint the pebble with clear varnish,' said Mr. Gruber. 'This makes it very shiny and stops the paint rubbing off.' Paddington thought this would make a very good present for Mr. Brown. He could use it as a paperweight.

'It will stop important papers blowing off his desk,' agreed Mr. Gruber.

Mr. Gruber then produced a pebble with a hole in it. He outlined the hole in red, added eyes, a nose and some hair. And there was a funny face!

If you can't find pebbles that give you ideas, you can make a pretty paperweight or ornament from a plain round pebble painted with a bright pattern.

On his next visit to Brightsea, Paddington found a pebble that was just the right shape for a model of his Aunt Lucy in her bowler hat and colorful poncho.

Mr. Gruber thought Paddington could also have saved money on the picture postcard he sent to Aunt Lucy.

'After all,' he said, 'she must have quite a lot of postcards of Brightsea by now. You could send her a truly original postcard using real Brightsea sand.'

You need: a plain postcard; glue or paste; a brush; fine sand.

What to do:
With the brush, paint a pattern on the card. At once cover the postcard with sand. Shake off any loose sand. You will be left with a sand-patterned postcard. Paddington decided to send his Aunt Lucy a postcard with a sand paw-mark on it.

'She will know at once who it's from,' he explained.

'If it's going all the way to Darkest Peru,' said Mr. Gruber, 'it would be a good idea to spray your finished card with clear varnish, so that the sand doesn't rub off.'

PADDINGTON CHUNKS

'Won't take a minute, sir,' said the photographer, disappearing behind a black cloth at the back of the camera. 'Just watch the birdie.'

Paddington looked around. There was no bird in sight as far as he could see. He went round behind the man and tapped him. The photographer, who appeared to be looking for something, jumped and then emerged from under his cloth. 'How do you expect me to take your picture if you don't stand in front? Now I've wasted a plate, and'—he looked shiftily at Paddington—'that will cost you a shilling!'

Paddington gave him a hard stare. 'You said there was a bird,' he said. 'And there wasn't.'

'I expect it flew away when it saw your face,' said the man nastily. 'Now where's my shilling?'

Paddington looked at him even harder for a moment. 'Perhaps the bird took it when it flew away,' he said.

from *A Bear Called Paddington*

But it was as he peered at the last item that a strange expression suddenly came over Paddington's face. He breathed heavily on his glasses several times, polished them with a piece of rag which he got from his suitcase, and then looked through them again at the board.

'That's called a selection from Schubert's *Unfinished Symphony*,' explained Judy in a whisper.

'What!' exclaimed Paddington hotly as his worst suspicions were confirmed. 'Mr. Gruber's paid sixpence each for our tickets and they haven't even finished it!'

from *Paddington At Large*

22

'Come along, Paddington,' Mr. Brown called, as the waiter set light to the pan. 'Come and see Mr. Gruber's omelette. It's on fire.'

'What!' cried Paddington, poking his head out from beneath the table. 'Mr. Gruber's omelette's on fire?'

He stared in astonishment at the waiter as he bore the silver tray with its flaming omelette towards the table.

'It's all right, Mr. Gruber,' he called, waving his paws in the air. 'I'm coming!'

Before the Browns could stop him, Paddington had grabbed his paw bowl and had thrown the contents over the tray. There was a loud hissing noise and before the astonished gaze of the waiter Mr. Gruber's omelette slowly collapsed into a soggy mess in the bottom of the dish.

Several people near the Browns applauded. 'What an unusual idea,' said one of them. 'Having the cabaret act sit at one of the tables just like anyone else.'

from *Paddington Helps Out*

'I thought you said that bear was going to the Peruvian Embassy?' exclaimed the bus conductor.

'The Peruvian Embassy?' repeated Mrs. Brown indignantly. 'We certainly said no such thing.'

'But you said she was C.D.,' broke in the Inspector. 'That stands for *Corps Diplomatique*, and people in the Diplomatic Corps are entitled to special treatment. That's why we brought her here.'

'No,' said Mrs. Bird, as light began to dawn. 'We didn't say C.D. We simply said she was feeling *seedy*. That's quite a different matter.'

from *Paddington On Top*

Paddington sat up in bed holding a thermometer in his paw. 'I think I must have caught the measles, Mrs. Bird,' he announced weakly. 'My temperature's over one hundred and twenty!'

'One hundred and twenty!' Mrs. Bird hurriedly examined the thermometer. 'That's not a temperature,' she exclaimed with relief. 'That's a marmalade stain.'

from *Paddington At Work*

Perhaps it is your birthday soon and you are planning to have a party. Why not make some of Mrs. Brown's delicious gingerbread bears? They are quite simple to make. Paddington says the cutting-out part is a bit difficult with paws, but it doesn't matter if the bears are not all exactly alike. In fact, they really look more lifelike if they are all a little bit different. You should ask a grown-up to put the bears in the oven and take them out for you, as hot ovens have a nasty habit of burning paws or hands.

Tools
1 large baking tray
1 teaspoon
1 tablespoon
1 sieve
1 mixing bowl
1 round-topped knife
1 rolling pin
1 pastry brush
1 wire cooling rack
kitchen scales
1 cup or small bowl
icing piping bag with a fine nozzle

You need:
(for about 10 bears)
200 grams (8 oz) self-raising flour
1 level teaspoon salt
2 level teaspoons ground ginger
1 level teaspoon mixed spice
100 grams (4 oz) white cooking fat
75 grams (3 oz) soft brown sugar
3 tablespoons cold milk
a little extra milk
icing sugar

Method

1. Make sure there is a shelf placed just above the middle of the oven.

2. Heat the oven to moderately hot (set it about 400°F). Grease the baking tray.

3. Shake flour, salt, ginger and spice through the sieve into the mixing bowl.

4. Add the fat and cut it into the dry ingredients with the round-topped knife until it is in very small pieces. Now rub it in with (clean!) fingertips.

5. Add the sugar.

6. Add the milk and, using the knife, mix the ingredients to a fairly stiff dough. Draw the pieces together with your fingertips.

7. Put the dough onto a working surface dusted with flour, and shape it into a ball with your hands.

8. Roll out fairly thinly with a floured rolling pin.

9. Cut out gingerbread bears with the round-topped knife, as shown.

10. Gather together the trimmings. Roll out again and cut out more bears. Put all the bears on the greased tray. Brush with a little extra milk.

11. Bake in the oven for about 15 minutes, until the bears are golden brown. Ask a grown-up to take the tray out of the oven.

12. Leave the bears on the tray for about 10 minutes, and then carefully lift them onto a wire rack to cool.

To decorate

When completely cool, prepare your icing. Half fill a cup or small bowl with icing sugar, shaken through a sieve. Add cold water—a few drops at a time—and mix with the round-topped knife until quite smooth, not too thick and not too runny. (Paddington says this is the most difficult stage, and it is a good idea to keep tasting the icing.) When the icing is ready, fill the icing bag. Using a fine nozzle, pipe eyes, a snout and a mouth on each gingerbread bear. Now pipe the outline of a label round each bear's neck. For a really original 'finishing touch', pipe a friend's initials on each label. Then you can use the bears as place markers at your party. And, of course, you can eat them as well!

HEAVENS ABOVE

Did you know that the sign of the Zodiac you were born under can play a large part in making you the type of person you are? Paddington has been studying the characteristics of each sign and trying to guess which ones all the people he knows were born under. Of course, Paddington has two birthdays each year, so he doesn't fit into any one category. But then, as everyone knows, Paddington is in a class of his own!

CAPRICORN (21 December–19 January)
You are ambitious and know exactly where you're going. People often think you are very serious, but you have your own kind of straight-faced humor. You make a very loyal friend and have great strength of character. You never let yourself be hurried. And you have a well-earned reputation for making ends meet.

AQUARIUS (20 January–18 February)
You are always interested in what is new—new friends, new places to go and things to do. You can easily give the impression of being aloof and stand-offish. But you are probably deep in thought, thinking up some new adventure.

PISCES (19 February–20 March)
Your lively wit makes you popular, although you have a rather annoying habit of changing your mind every two minutes. You sometimes give the impression of being shy. But once you have finally made up your mind about something, you astound others by your self-confidence in putting your ideas across.

ARIES (21 March–20 April)
You are impulsive—you like to do things on the spur of the moment. But you do lack patience with those who don't want to drop everything and join you! You have a lot of energy, coupled with great perseverance. Once you have made up your mind to do something you won't stop until it's done. You can lack flexibility.

TAURUS (21 April–20 May)
You love luxury and want the best of everything. You enjoy good food. You are happiest doing things with your family and friends, rather than alone. You nearly always have very strong ideas about exactly what shape your life should take. Your strength of mind is sometimes called 'stubbornness' by other people. And you are very practical.

GEMINI (21 May–20 June)
You have a very happy-go-lucky nature. This makes you great fun to have around, although some of your more gloomy friends may get a bit tired of your eternal cheerfulness! You are very resourceful. You have to guard against people taking advantage of your good nature. But, even if they do, you are very resilient.

CANCER (21 June–20 July)
You have a tendency to live in the past. You are gentle by nature and will do almost anything to avoid an argument. You have very strong intuitions and may even be psychic! You are artistic and creative, and usually go out of your way to make your surroundings warm and colorful.

LEO (21 July–21 August)
You have a very strong, powerful personality and can easily be thought arrogant or vain. You have a lot of energy and drive. Instead of waiting for things to happen you go out and *make* them happen. You are very optimistic and are always prepared to give your friends the benefit of the doubt. And you are very generous.

VIRGO (22 August–22 September)

You tend on the whole to be very prudent. But when you feel like it you can make very extravagant gestures. You are slow to make friends because you are shy of taking the first step. But once you make a friend, you stay friends for life! You may well have a great love of books. And you are very critical.

SCORPIO (23 October–22 November)

You have a strong sense of humor which enables you to get over any disappointments. You can give the impression of being secretive and you don't like always to be part of a crowd. You are a wonderful friend and a bad enemy —you don't go in for half measures. You could turn out to be a Saint or a Sinner.

LIBRA (23 September–22 October)

You love harmony and get on well with other people. You don't like being alone. You like nice surroundings and have very strong feelings about the sort of clothes you like to wear. You may be an escapist, loving to dream up a fantasy world of your own. And you often put off things you have to do in the real world— almost indefinitely!

SAGITTARIUS (23 November– 20 December)

You are definitely a 'doer'—which means that you are sometimes thought to be impatient. You are very independent and like to dash off after your own pursuits. Your zest for life makes you want to pass on some of your enthusiasm to those younger than yourself. You love travelling and feel very at home in far-flung places.

Pawprints

Here are the pawprints made by some animals, which you might spot in soil, sand or snow.

Otter

Badger

Deer

Rabbit

31

All Is Revealed

Paddington has been looking at an old book he found in the Browns' bookcase called *Fortune Telling. The Secrets of the Orient Revealed.* If you cross his paw with silver, he may reveal some of the secrets to you too.

Reading cups

This is very interesting because tea leaves always make quite different patterns. When you have only the dregs left in your teacup, swirl them round three times. Now quickly turn the cup upside down onto the saucer. Of course it doesn't work if you make your tea with bags. Paddington tried it once with the cocoa grounds left in the bottom of his mug, but the only 'message' he got was a rather fierce one from Mrs. Bird when she saw the tablecloth!

The tea leaves make various shapes inside the cup. The nearer to the rim of the cup the shapes are, the sooner the things they predict will happen. Here is a useful list of shapes and what they mean. Initials stand for people you know.

Ace   change
Anchor   a journey
Arrow   danger
Balloon   good luck if it's going up: bad luck if it's coming down. (And it's cheating to turn the cup upside down and give it a thump on the bottom!)
Basket   present or visitor (both if you're lucky!)
Bee   hard work
Beehive   good luck
Bird   good news
Candle   help is on its way
Cat   watch out for someone doing you a bad turn
Clouds   trouble
Cup   a reward
Dog   a good friend
Egg   new scheme—you're hatching a new idea!
Envelope   news
Flag   news from far away
Flower   you get something you've asked for
Gate   happiness
Glove   a challenge; someone is throwing down the gauntlet!
Gun   trouble to be avoided
Hammer   work
Key   a new project
Kite   a wish will be granted
Knife   you may fall out with a friend
Ladder   success
Lion   a quarrel
Moon   riches
Mountain   an obstacle in your path
Music notes   good luck
Owl   bad luck

Parrot   gossip
Profile   new friend
Sailor   someone is coming home
Ship   travel—with something gained at the end of it
Spider   reward for work done
Star   very lucky: health, wealth and happiness
Tent   you'll wander
Tree   happiness
Violin   independence
Waterfall   a sign of plenty
Window   your happiness is at home
X   someone upsets you
Zebra   foreign travel

So, if Paddington's teacup looked like this . . .

It is likely that he would receive a postcard from Aunt Lucy (flag: news from far away near her initial); make a new friend (profile), come into some unexpected bun money (moon: riches), and he should be very careful where he puts any new marmalade stains, or he could end up in trouble with Mrs. Bird (gun: trouble to be avoided).

Reading cards

According to fortune tellers, each card in a pack has a meaning, and can be used to foretell the future. Shuffle the pack well. Ask the person whose fortune is to be told to cut the pack seven times. Then arrange the top seven cards in a line and 'read' them with the meanings given below as a guide. Try to link up the meanings of the seven cards, rather than just reading each one in isolation.

Hearts

Ace   a gift from a friend
2   a visit from a friend
3   useful advice is on its way
4   you have plans to improve your surroundings
5   an invitation
6   a special outing
7   travel plans
8   look out for a friend who is envious of something you've got
9   someone far away gets in touch
10   someone shows appreciation of you by giving you a present
Jack   a stranger brings excitement into your life
Queen   a mother, an aunt, a teacher (or some other woman) is very helpful with one of your schemes
King   you can turn to some older man, in a position of authority, for advice

Diamonds

Ace   good advice leads to a gain
2   it will help you to discuss any money problems with family and friends
3   people don't appreciate you
4   beware of extravagance!
5   a trip or outing gives you lots of opportunities for spending
6   something you make brings money
7   a windfall from an older person
8   you need some extra money. Don't be shy about asking for it
9   take a chance: it will pay off
10   act quickly and make a gain
Jack   a stranger, whom you will soon meet, will be very lucky for you where money is concerned
Queen   an older woman will help you with a practical problem
King   an older man gives you the opportunity to earn some spare cash

Spades

Ace there are problems ahead; don't take any risks

2 be very cautious

3 you will be involved in a quarrel

4 be very careful whose advice you take

5 don't listen to gossip

6 a minor setback in one of your plans

7 don't be jealous: it will only harm yourself

8 don't take any important decisions just now; wait a while

9 you will get a letter soon which will help you make up your mind about something

10 after a lot of delays you will finally achieve what you want

Jack someone is having a bad influence on you

Queen some woman you know is unlucky for you

King some man whom you trust and look up to is not a real friend

Clubs

Ace temporary delays in something you've planned

2 you make a mistake in something

3 you will change your mind about something

4 you should concentrate on your home and family just now

5 don't rush into something

6 a bit of dull plodding is necessary at this time

7 don't be afraid to try something new: you'll be very successful

8 have some patience: something you're hoping for will happen soon

9 look after your belongings: there is a danger of losing something

10 plans for your future are taking shape

Jack someone you know tries to persuade you to go on a holiday or trip. You will enjoy it if you go.

Queen a very good friend will help you out of difficulties

King a man will come to the rescue during a dull or unhappy period

These are the cards which Paddington chose. Can you tell what his fortune is to be?

SEEING STARS

One morning when Paddington stopped off at Mr. Gruber's shop in the Portobello Road for his usual cocoa and buns, he found his friend hard at work. He was polishing what looked like a long, heavy tube. 'Is it snack time already, Mr. Brown?' asked Mr. Gruber, stopping for a rest and mopping his brow absent-mindedly with a large duster. 'I bought this old brass telescope at an auction yesterday and it needs a good rub.' He went off to get the cocoa mugs. 'If you would like to borrow the telescope tonight,' said Mr. Gruber, reappearing with the tray, 'you can look through it and see a Great Bear.' Paddington was so surprised he nearly fell off the horsehair sofa. But Mr. Gruber explained that the Great Bear was the name of a group of stars—or constellation. 'The Ancient Greeks gave the constellations the names by which they're still known today,' he said. 'Do the stars look like a bear?' asked Paddington. 'I suppose they do if you use a bit of imagination,' said Mr. Gruber, taking a dusty book down from a shelf behind him. While Paddington enjoyed his cocoa and put his paws up, Mr. Gruber made some notes and drawings on a large piece of paper. Here are some of the things he showed Paddington.

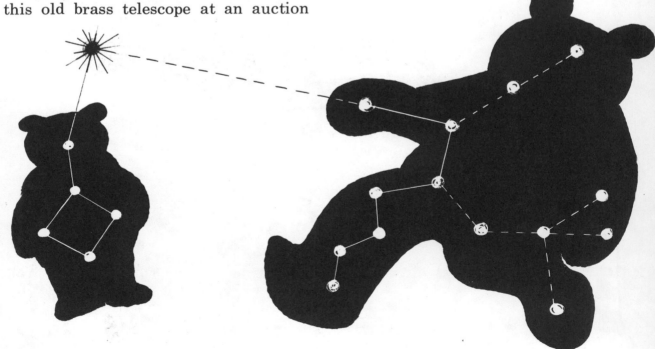

Although all the stars appear to move about the sky, there is one star—called the Pole Star—which appears to remain still. This star shows the direction of the North Pole. If you live north of the Equator you can easily find the Pole Star. It is part of a group of stars called the Little Bear. The easiest way to find the Pole Star is to look for the Plow, which is part of the Great Bear. If you follow an imaginary line from the two end stars of the Plow you come to the Pole Star. If you can find the Pole Star you will always know which direction is North. So you should never get lost.

Paddington says it's quite easy to get lost, even if you do know where North is; especially if you've set out for somewhere, stopped for a quick snack and forgotten the address!

This is the view of the night sky Paddington's Aunt Lucy has from her room in the Home for Retired Bears in Lima, Darkest Peru. You will have the same view if you live south of the Equator. Aunt Lucy can't see the Great Bear. But as she is surrounded by bears anyway, she doesn't really mind.

Paddington's 20 Questions

Choose the answer you think is correct, and count up your score at the end.

1 Paddington's favourite snack is:
a) toast and honey
b) chocolate pudding
c) marmalade sandwiches
d) treacle tart

2 Paddington has buns and cocoa with his friend Mr. Gruber:
a) at snack time
b) at afternoon tea time
c) on Saturday mornings
d) on Bank Holiday outings

3 Mr. Gruber calls Paddington:
a) Paddington
b) Paddy
c) Old Bear!
d) Mr. Brown

4 Paddington's Aunt Lucy lives in:
a) Australia
b) England
c) Peru
d) Mexico

5 Paddington's Aunt Lucy wears:
a) a sou'wester
b) a bowler hat
c) a sunbonnet
d) a woolly hat with a pom-pom

6 Paddington keeps notes:
a) in a diary
b) in a scrapbook
c) in an old exercise book
d) on a chart on his bedroom wall

7 The Incas—the ancient people of Peru—worshipped:
a) a huge golden statue of a bear
b) a beautiful goddess
c) the mountains
d) the sun

8 Paddington's hat was:
a) bought at Barkridge's Sale
b) an old one of Mr. Brown's
c) his Uncle's
d) a Christmas present from Mr. Gruber

9 Paddington's Aunt Lucy taught him:
a) a special hard stare
b) a double somersault
c) how to sing the Peruvian national anthem
d) how to make and embroider ponchos

10 The Browns' housekeeper is called:
a) Mrs. Fox
b) Mrs. Bird
c) Mrs. Bull
d) Mrs. Finch

11 Paddington wears:
a) a mackintosh
b) a cape
c) a duffle coat
d) a parka

12 To help him with his shopping, Paddington uses:
a) a basket on wheels
b) a suitcase
c) a string bag
d) an old carrier bag

13 The Browns first met Paddington:
a) on holiday in Peru
b) at the zoo
c) on the beach at Brightsea
d) outside the Lost Property office at Paddington Station

14 Paddington lives at:
a) 6 Portobello Road
b) 26 Victoria Place
c) 32 Windsor Gardens
d) 18 Railway Cuttings

15 How many birthdays does Paddington have each year?
a) 1
b) 2
c) 3
d) 4

16 Mr. Brown:
a) is a stationmaster
b) works in the City
c) owns a bunshop
d) has a stall in the Portobello Market

17 Paddington's Aunt Lucy sends him:
a) letters
b) telegrams
c) tape recordings
d) postcards

18 Mr. Curry, the Browns' next-door neighbor, is:
a) mean and bad-tempered
b) generous to a fault
c) very friendly—always popping in and out
d) extremely absent-minded

19 The capital of Darkest Peru is:
a) Stow-On-The-Wold
b) Santiago
c) Lima
d) Brussels

20 Paddington's very first adventure at the Browns' home was with:
a) a lawnmower
b) a bath
c) a pan of toffee
d) a vacuum cleaner

Answers:
1: c); **2:** a) ; **3:** d); **4:** c); **5:** b); **6:** b); **7:** d); **8:** c); **9:** a); **10:** b); **11:** c); **12:** a); **13:** d); **14:** c); **15:** b); **16:** b); **17:** d); **18:** a); **19:** c); **20:** b).

Score:
15–20: Excellent! Have a bun to celebrate.
10–15: Fair. Have half a bun!
Under 10: You've obviously still got quite a few of Paddington's adventures to find out about!

Room for Ideas

Paddington was busy scratching out the words 'At a lewse end' in his scrapbook, and was adding, in large capital letters, the ominous ones: 'DECKERATING MY NEW ROOM.' (*More About Paddington*)

Make Your Mark

You need:
a very large piece of white paper; ruler; pencil; felt-tip pens

What to do
Mark the paper into squares as shown. The simplest way to do this is to fold the paper in half a few times. If you fold the paper in half four times, pressing down on the folds each time, when you open it up you will have sixteen squares. Outline the squares with a ruler and pencil. Attach the paper to your bedroom wall. Keep some colored felt pens nearby. Whenever a friend comes to visit, ask him or her to 'decorate' a square—with a drawing, poem, joke or anything you like. In time you will have a very original poster.

Here are some ways in which you can brighten up the walls in your room, and your door—without any of the dire results which Paddington achieved when he tried his paw at decorating!

Family Tree

You need:
a large piece of cardboard; pencil; poster paints; photographs of your family—the older the better; double-sided sticky tape.

What to do
Draw a big tree on the cardboard. With fairly thick poster paint, color the trunk brown and the foliage a bright green. Leave it to dry. Collect photographs of your family and relatives as babies or young children. Fix these to the tree with small pieces of double-sided tape on the back. People should have fun trying to recognize who is who!

40

Picture

Most junk shops and second-hand record shops have dusty piles of old sheet music which you can buy very cheaply. Paddington's friend, Mr. Gruber, has a pile in his shop in the Portobello Road. The top sheets of popular songs usually have the title in lovely ornate lettering. If you look through these piles you can often find a title which looks attractive, or amusing, framed and hung on a wall.

Examples: 'Beautiful Dreamer' above a bed.
'You Were Never Lovelier' beside a mirror!
'Oh What a Beautiful Morning', or 'Stormy Weather' beside a window.

Nameplate

You need

a cardboard long enough to take your first name with letters about 7.5 centimeters (3 inches) high; a pile of old magazines and newspapers; scissors; pencil; rubber; glue; brightly-colored sticky tape.

What to do

Go through the pile of magazines and newspapers and cut out lots of letters for each letter in your first name. For example if your name is Judy you will cut out lots of Js Us Ds and Ys. Try to find letters in as many different sizes and colors as possible. Now draw the outline of the letters in your name on the card in pencil. Glue the cut-out letters inside the large letters as shown. Fill up the letters as closely as possible. When the glue is dry, carefully rub out the pencil outline. Frame the edges of the nameplate with brightly-colored sticky tape and add a little loop to the back of the sign with which to fix it to the outside of your door.

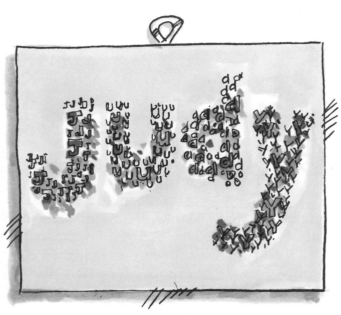

Fun for Kids

Perhaps you have a small brother or sister, or know some very young children. Here are some ideas which Paddington suggests might entertain them.

Shadow Show

Paddington says a Shadow Show is always popular—and is very good value as you don't need any special materials. All you need is a large piece of white paper stuck to the wall, or an area of white wall; a strong light (such as a big flashlight) which you shine on your 'screen'. You stand between the light and the screen. Before the show, practice some of the shapes shown here. Ducks and rabbits are always favorites with young children. With a little preparation, you can read a short story about Jemima Puddleduck or Brer Rabbit, and illustrate your story with shadow characters. (Ask at your local lending library for books about these two characters.) With practice you can present lots of different stories with a whole variety of animal characters.

Circular Paddington Jigsaw

You need
a large piece of white paper
a large piece of stiff cardboard
bright poster paints
a pencil
a pair of compasses
scissors and glue

What to do
Set your compasses to 10 centimeters (4 inches). Draw a pencil circle with them on both paper and cardboard. Then draw a picture of Paddington onto the paper, inside the circle. Don't forget his duffel coat, wellingtons and hat! Make the picture as big as possible. Now paint the picture with poster paints, mixed fairly thickly to give good strong colors. Fill in the background with a bright color, such as scarlet, making sure that every bit of the paper is covered. Leave until the paint dries. Then glue the paper on the cardboard. Make sure it fits exactly. (If necessary, trim the cardboard.) Now draw a simple jigsaw design on top. Next cut along the lines of your design to make the jigsaw pieces. Be very careful not to snip off any edges or the pieces won't fit. For a special finish, paint the pieces with clear varnish.

Bubbles
Young children love chasing bubbles and trying to catch them. You can make your own bubble kit.

You need:
a small clean screw-top jar (such as an old peanut butter jar)
liquid soap or detergent
some wire

What to do
Put a couple of generous squeezes of the liquid detergent into the jar. Add water until the jar is about two-thirds full of the mixture. Put the top on and shake gently. Bend the wire into the shape shown here. Make sure that the bigger loop is not too big to go through the neck of the jar. Twist the ends of the loops round the stem so that there are no sharp edges sticking out. To make bubbles, simply dip the wire loop into the mixture, take it out, and blow gently through the loop.

Paddington Mobile

This is something which will appeal to the very youngest children. Even babies get bored, and a Paddington Mobile will keep them amused for hours.

You need:

3 pieces of strong wire, each 10 centimeters (4 inches) long
1 piece of wire, 15 centimeters (6 inches) long (Ask a grown-up to cut these lengths for you.)
transparent nylon thread or fishing gut
fine stiff card
poster paints
pencil and scissors
clear varnish and a brush

What to do

Draw five shapes on the cardboard. They should all be roughly the same size (about 7.5 centimeters, 3 inches across). For example, you could draw: a bun with icing and a cherry on top; a shiny wellington boot; a bright red P for Paddington; a jar of marmalade; Paddington's hat.

Cut out the shapes. Paint them with thick poster paints, on *both* sides (letting one side dry before you do the other side). When the paint is dry, paint your shapes again with clear varnish. Make a small hole at the top of each shape. Attach a length of nylon thread or fish line to each, then tie them to the ends of the pieces of wire. Attach a long piece of thread to the top piece of wire with a strong knot. Your mobile probably won't hang properly at first, but you can slide the knots from side to side until it is all balanced. Hang the mobile where the baby can see it easily as it moves gently in the air.

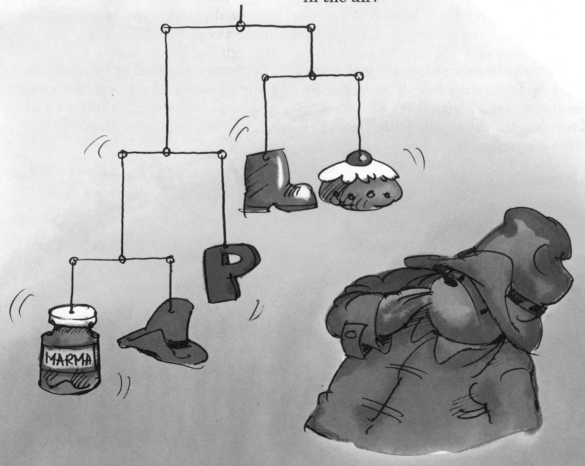

44

Getting Ahead

The **Legionbear** has gone off to a life of adventure in the desert. He has left all behind him—except an emergency supply of marmalade sandwiches, of course!

The **Astrobear** zooms through space on his special mission. When he puts the first pawprint on the moon, it will be a small step for Astrobear, but a giant leap for all Earthbears.

The **Highwaybear** was notorious for his sudden raids on coaches. The unhappy passengers were made to 'stand and deliver' all the buns they had brought for the journey.

The **Swagbear** camps by a billabong. He keeps a wary eye open for kangaroos, which might swipe his billycan of cocoa. They would be told to hop it!

45

The **Bear Musketeers** fought duels to defend their king from all his enemies. To be chosen as a Musketeer was a real feather in any bear's cap.

The **Incabear** lived long ago in darkest Peru, high up in the Andes mountains. Aunt Lucy is very envious of Incabear's splendid hat of gold.

Beau Bear is very proud of his large wardrobe of fine clothes. He employs a valetbear specially to remove marmalade stains from his breeches.

PADDINGTON'S GREAT TRAIN RACE

A Board Game for 2–4 Players

For this game you need:
dice
a shaker (an eggcup will do)
up to 4 counters (you can make your own; see foot of page)

The object of the game is to be first in a race from START to the station at the end of your line. Two, three or four can play. Each player has a different color, yellow, green, red or blue. Place your counter on the first square of your color, where it says START.

Take it in turns to throw the dice. Remember: you must throw a six to start.

When you have thrown a six, throw again right away, and move forward the number of squares shown by the dice (for example, if you throw a three, move forward three squares).

On each track there is a square with an 'obstacle'. If you land here, you must go back to START. Then wait your turn to play again—at least you don't have to throw a six this time to get re-started!

Once you are through the smoke from Mr. Curry's bonfire, you will see ahead that the tracks cross. If you land on the square where the tracks cross, go back to the square *just before the smoke*. Then wait your turn and start again from there. To finish, you must throw the *exact* number needed. The first person to reach home is the winner.

The Counters

To make your own counters, draw a circle about 2 centimeters ($\frac{3}{4}$ inch) in diameter on a piece of cardboard, and cut it out. Perhaps you can find a coin the right size. Draw round it to make your circle. You need one counter for each player. You should make four for this game. Paint them in bright colors—red, green, yellow and blue.

FINISH

FINISH

FINISH

FINISH

Most people, especially children, love a puppet show. It can be even more fun if you put on the show yourselves. You can make the puppets, build the theater, and even write a 'play' for your puppets to perform. Here are some ideas to get you started. There is a short play using the characters here, on pages 54 and 55.

You need:

strong cardboard   sticky tape
paints or crayons   tracing paper
sticks   a pencil and scissors

To make the puppets
To give you some practice, here are four 'shapes'—Paddington, Mr. Brown, Mrs. Brown and Aunt Lucy. Don't cut these out of the book—you'll want them again, or someone else will want them. Instead trace around the shapes, stick your tracing paper onto cardboard, then cut the shape out of the cardboard. Paint the characters as has been done here. Now attach a stick to the *back* of each puppet with sticky tape, as shown. Remember

to leave enough stick for your hand to hold comfortably. Once you've got the hang of making stick puppets this way, you can make them any size or shape you like. They can be people or animals. You can start by tracing them from pictures in magazines, for example, or you can draw your character straight onto the cardboard.

To make the theater
You can make your theater to any design you like. It is just a large cardboard, with the middle cut out. (Remember that the 'arch' over the 'stage' must be big enough for the puppets to appear in.) You can decorate the edges which the audience sees, for example, making it look as though there are curtains hanging at the sides. Cut strips of cardboard for supports and put your theater at the edge of a table (as shown on page 55). You then kneel or sit behind the table and work the puppets from below. Put a cloth on the table to hide you from the audience. Don't let the audience see your hands.

PADDINGTON.

Aunt Lucy.

Mr. Brown.

Mrs. Brown.

The Play

Paddington enters. He looks around the 'stage' and then peers at the audience.

Paddington	That's strange. (He makes counting movements) One, two, three . . . four, five, six . . . seventeen, eighteen, nineteen . . . take away four . . . add ten . . . That's *very strange*. It's definitely June the twenty-fifth today. My summer birthday . . . (to audience) bears have *two* birthdays a year, you know. And yet . . . there's no-one here. *Mr. Brown enters.*
Mr. Brown	Morning Paddington.
Paddington	Hello, Mr. Brown. I . . .
Mr. Brown	Sorry I can't stop. I have something special to do. *Mr. Brown exits.*
Paddington	Oh! Oh, well, I expect he's got a lot on his mind. (darkly to audience) Trouble at the office! *Mrs. Brown enters.*

54

Mrs. Brown	Oh! Oh, there you are, Paddington. Er . . . goodbye.	**Aunt Lucy**	Paddington!
		Paddington	Aunt Lucy!
	Mrs. Brown exits.	**Mr. Brown**	We thought you'd be
Paddington	(nearly falls over back-	. .	surprised. She's come
	wards with surprise)		all the way from Lima
	Goodbye!		by courtesy of the
	Don't say Mrs. Brown's		Home for Retired Bears.
	forgotten what day it is		They had a special fête
	too.		to raise the money
	SONG (OFF) Sung by		for her fare.
	Mr. and Mrs. Brown	**Mrs. Brown**	What do you say to
	and Aunt Lucy.		that, Paddington?
	Happy birthday to you.	**Paddington**	I think (pauses) I think
	Happy birthday to you.		it's the nicest birthday
	Happy birthday, dear		I very nearly didn't
	Paddington,		have, Mrs. Brown.
	Happy birthday to you.		
	Mr. and Mrs. Brown		THE END
	enter accompanied by		
	Aunt Lucy.		

WELL CHOSEN WORDS

You can get a lot of fun just from cutting pictures and words from old newspapers and magazines. The secret is to choose words and pictures which aren't meant to go together! Then you stick them onto a piece of paper so that it looks as though they do. For example, here is a picture of a marmot. It isn't very likely that he would be saying 'Here is the News' as he is here.

You can use pictures of people or animals. There are some more examples on the next page to give you ideas.

MAKE A COLLECTION

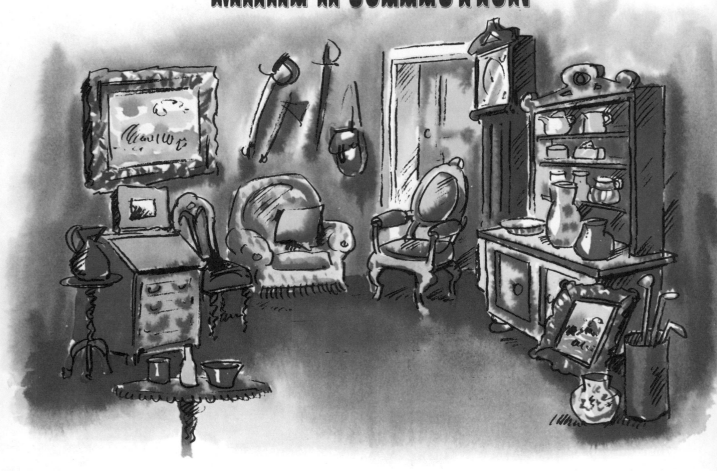

Mr. Gruber's shop in the Portobello Road is crammed full of antiques and junk. He often has people coming in to look for something they specially collect —from copper kettles to old marmalade jars! Making a collection can be great fun. It is best to have a theme, or to build your collection round one type of thing. Then if you start collecting— jugs, for example, you will probably find that friends start looking out for unusual ones to give you as Christmas or birthday presents. Here are some ideas which Mr. Gruber suggests might start you off.

Shells and pebbles

These are good to collect, and they are free! Look out for unusual shapes and colors. When you have a fair number collected, the best way to display them is in water. Wash them, then put them in a glass bowl (an old fish bowl is ideal), and cover them with water.

Bears

Collect all sorts of bears, and display them on a shelf. Perhaps you already have an old teddy bear. Look out for wooden bears, chocolate bears, glass bears, glove puppet bears, embroidered bears, stamps with bears on, books about bears (like Rupert and Winnie-The-Pooh, as well as Paddington).

Postcards

Paddington collects postcards and sticks them in his scrapbook. You can display postcards by covering a panel of a door or cupboard with felt. Then criss-cross it with colored tape. Secure the tape where it crosses with drawing pins. Now you can arrange the postcards as shown. Look out for old postcards with embroidered silk pictures, old photograph postcards of the area you live in, funny seaside postcards, children's postcards, postcards of famous places you visit, postcards of favorite paintings (you can get these at art galleries and museums). And, of course, ask all your friends to be sure to send you postcards from their holidays.

59

Jigsaws

Collect old jigsaws, circular jigsaws, simple wooden jigsaws. Collect jigsaws with a theme—map jigsaws or wildlife jigsaws (showing birds or butterflies, for example). A good way to display jigsaws is to stick the finished puzzles onto cardboard, and hang them on the wall.

Keys

Look in junk shops, and ask all your friends for old keys. Try to get as many different sizes and designs as possible. Polish up brass keys. Paint old metal keys glossy black. When you have a really big collection, hang them from little hooks set into a pegboard as shown. Arrange them in rows from the largest to the smallest, or in a pattern of your choice.

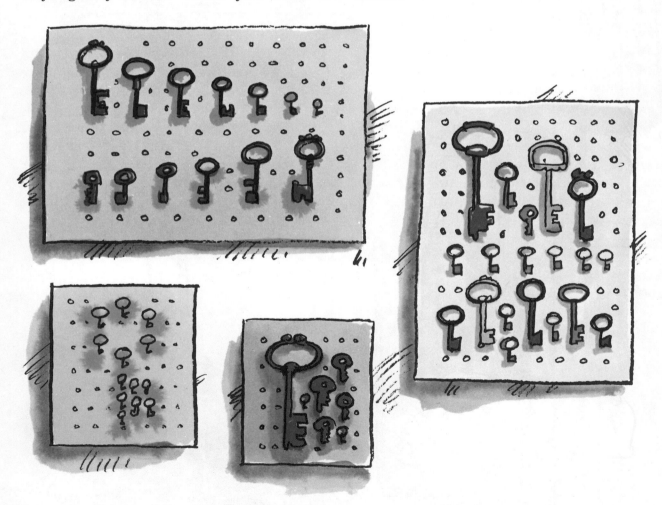